LEARNING ENGINEERED
P U B L I S H I N G

FOR MITCHELL CHRISTIAN DICKINSON

HELLO SUNSHINE!

HELLO RAIN!

HELLO EARTH!

HELLO CRANE!

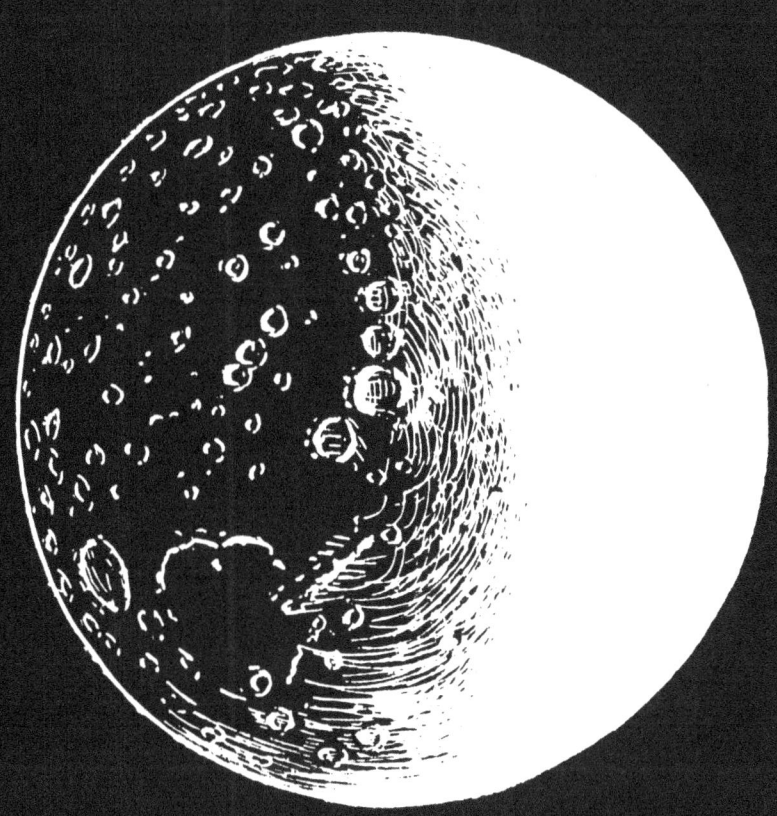

HELLO MOON!

HELLO BIRD!

HELLO BEAR!

HELLO HERD!

HELLO MOM!

HELLO CRIB!

HELLO DAD!

HELLO BIB!

HELLO ROCKER!

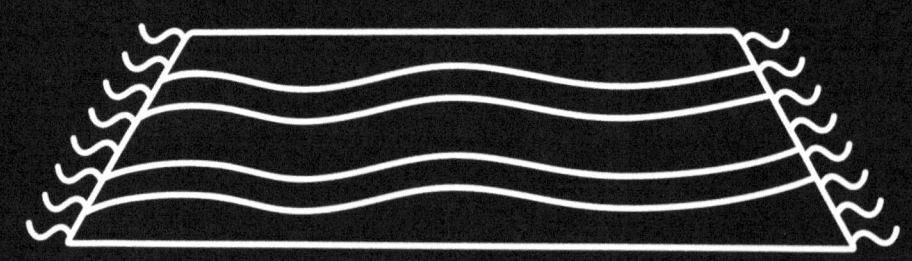

HELLO RUG!

HELLO BED!

HELLO BUG!

HELLO FLOWER!

HELLO SHOE!

HELLO TREE!

HELLO YOU!

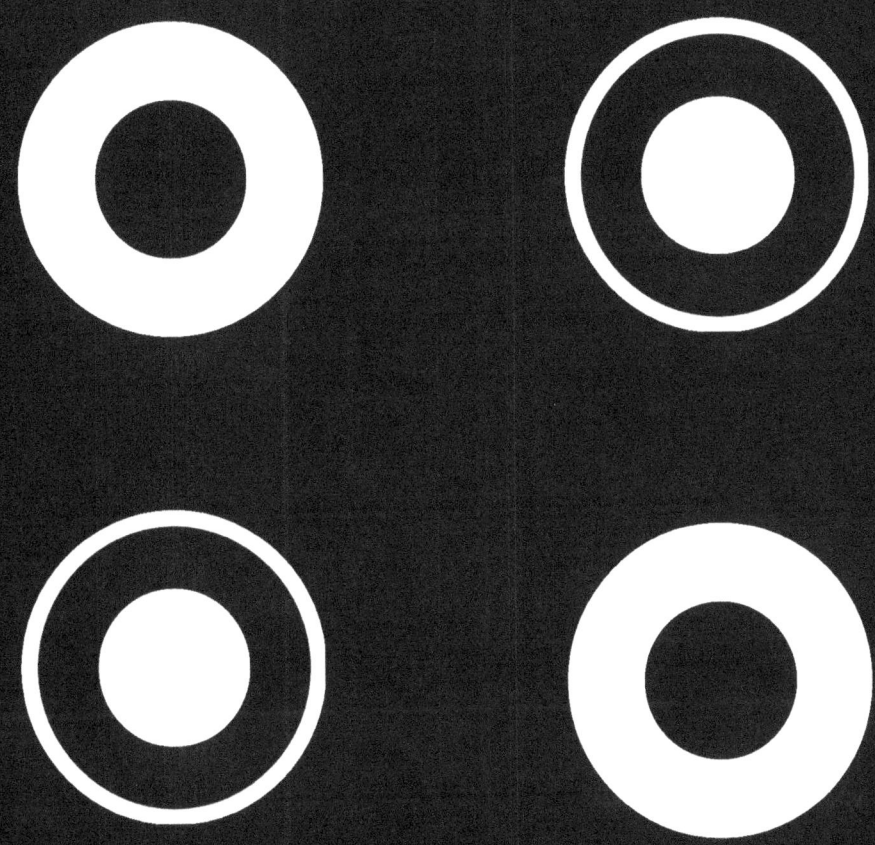

CONCENTRIC CIRCLES

COLLECT ALL THE HELLO CONTRAST! BOOKS!